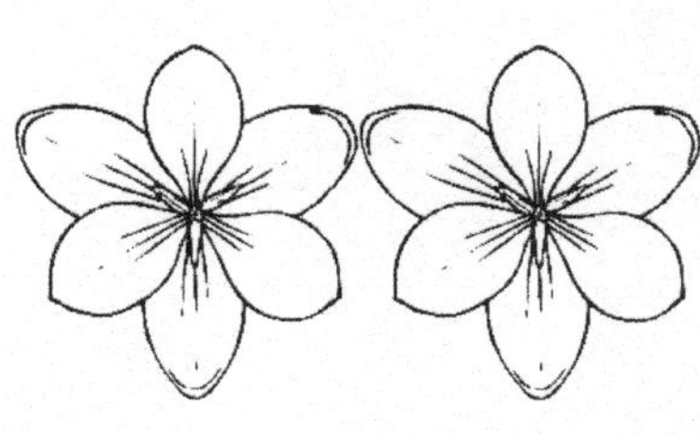

Monday Morning Devotions

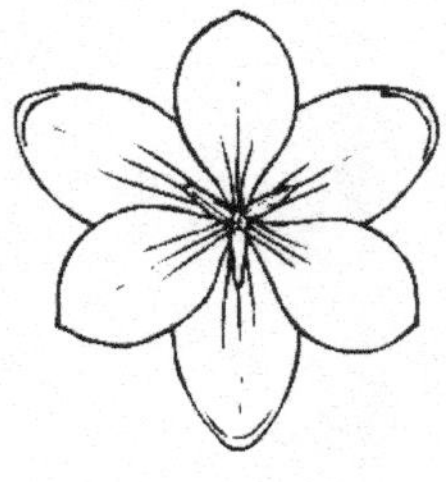

Monday Morning Devotions

Sandra Lee Cleary

ISBN Paperback: 978-1-941516-65-2

Contact the author at SandraLeeCleary@gmail.com

Website: https://journeythroughourbranches.com/

Editor: Judy Sheer Watters

Scripture quotations marked NLT are from the New Living Translation. Copyright © 1996, 2004,2007 by Tyndale House Publishers, Inc. Carol Stream, Illinois 60188. All rights reserved.

This book was printed in the United States of America

INTRODUCTION

Growing in the Christian life we are to be in God's Word each day—to let Him guide our every day and thoughts. If you are a new Christian, you tell yourself I don't have time or I'm too busy to do that. You might add a daily devotional to your magazine rack located in your library (aka the family restroom).

I am not a new Christian as I gave my heart to the Lord when I was sixteen. There are periods in my life I do not feel I gave Him all I should have given Him. But He has never left my side. I have felt His presence, oh, so many times. As life goes on, we slide a bit. We don't like to think we do, but we are still human, and we will step out of line. We live in a sin-marred world. We cannot get around that.

What I've tried to do with my *Monday Morning Devotions is* to give you and me a few moments on Monday, before we start the day to take time for God. To Praise Him and reflect what He has done for us. It only takes five minutes for a quick read to let the verses resound in our minds all day. Most of my devotionals have come from my own life experiences. Maybe you will see something similar in your life and it will give you some help. That is my prayer for each of you.

First and foremost, thank you to my husband for his patience with me as I sit in my office working diligently on the computer. He is my utmost supporter.

I must thank my dearest friend and ex-business partner, Judy Watters for all her help with formatting and her encouragement. I've leaned on her a lot in all the years I've known her. She is an inspiration to all she works with.

Another big thank you goes to my dear friends in the Christian Writers Group of Greater San Antonio, Cathey Edgington, Terry Beard, Monica Clegg, Al Bates, Laverne Stanley, Nancy Christy, April Gardner, Randall Hays, Tina McDonald, Jim Hopper, and Paul

Lane. And my dear friend Brenda Blanchard who encouraged me to join the group twenty years ago. Thank you.

My plan, as slow as I am, is to work on another book for one devotional a week for an entire year. Whatever God has in plan for me, that is what my plan is, but I'm not sure yet what my Savior's plan is. His plan is always better than mine. I just need to be still and listen. To God be the glory.

Romans 3:23

For all have sinned and fall short of the glory of God. (NIV)

In the morning, LORD,

you hear my voice;

in the morning I lay my requests

before you and wait expectantly.

Psalm 5:3 NIV

TRUST

Trust in the Lord always, for the Lord God is the eternal Rock.
Isaiah 26:4 (NLT)

One morning while watching the Today program, they showed how the F18 Hornets land on the aircraft carrier George H.W. Bush. Amy Robach, a journalist, had a front row view as she rode in the back seat of the cockpit.

I watched in awe as they took off from the carrier. It was as if they were catapulted into the air from a giant slingshot. The pilot circled the carrier then proceeded to bring the plane in to land, and as they touched down, the hook grabbed the plane to bring it to a sudden stop. They said it was like a controlled car crash going from 180 to zero.

Each person aboard that carrier has 100% trust in each other to bring the plane in safely. Without that trust there would be mishaps, maybe even deaths.

Proverbs 3:26 says: “For the Lord will be your confidence and will keep your foot from being caught.” He is telling us to trust in Him, and He will take care of us. To let go of our problems, concerns, and fears. He has us in His hands always and will always be there when we cry out for help. We just need to give everything over to Him to take care of. Trust in God for all things, big or small. He is our Rock.

Dear Heavenly Father, I pray you take all my worries in Your hands. Amen.

My Talks with God

REPRIMAND

The mountains quaked at the presence of the Lord. The God of Mount Sinai, in the presence of the Lord, the God of Israel.
Judges 5:5 (NLT)

Raising children can be exasperating sometimes. You're the adult, so you try to guide your child to choose the right path. This doesn't always work, especially if you have a strong-willed child. You can only imagine how God feels when He sees His children take the wrong path. The book of Judges tells us of disobedient and idolatrous people, and how they are defeated time and time again because of their rebellion against God. He raised up an army to throw off the bondage and restore the nation to worship. Even so, they reverted to their old sin nature. Angered with Israel, as stated in Judges 2:20-21 (NAS), "Because this nation has transgressed My covenant which I commanded their fathers, and has not listened to My voice, I also will no longer drive out before them any of the nations which Joshua left when He died."

Our God is a loving God who wants the best for each one of His children, but you cannot continue to turn your back on Him. He is a just God. In the end, God wants us to ask for forgiveness, just as you want your child to ask you to forgive them when they have done wrong. You make rules in your house as God makes rules for us to live by. All He wants is to live with His children in harmony and peace.

Dear Father, forgive me when I let You down. Amen.

My Talks with God

SATAN TAKE A HIKE

"Get behind Me, Satan! You are a stumbling block to Me; for you are not setting your mind on God's interests, but man's."
Matthew 16:23 (NASB)

These words are printed on my mind, especially when I go out shopping. Mind you, I love to shop just like any other woman. The bargains, oh my. I can save so much. But when I get home and realize how much money I spent, I'm remorseful. I'm not alone in this. Every day each one of us is tempted by Satan in one way or another. Whether it's shopping, eating, or doing something that goes beyond our nature. Satan is always there to entice us. "Go ahead, you deserve it," or "Who's going to know?"

Satan tempted Christ in Luke 4 (NASB). The Evil One painted a beautiful picture for Christ. "I will give You all this domain and its glory, for it has been handed over to me, and I give it to whomever I wish." Satan always has an answer for everything.

Jesus replied in the same scripture saying, "It is written, you shall worship the Lord your God and serve Him only."

With God's help, I will continue to seek God's guidance and tell Satan, "Take a hike."

Gracious Heavenly Father, I ask for Your guidance every day in all I do and say. May you keep Satan far from me. Amen.

My Talks with God

COURAGE

On the day I called Thou didst answer me; Thou didst make me bold with strength in my soul. Psalm 138:3 (NASB)

All my life I've tried to avoid conflict. I do not like arguing, and most of all, I do not like to fight. I don't understand why some like to provoke others into physical altercations. I remember asking my mother, "Why do people have to be so mean to each other?"

Many times, I've avoided confronting someone guilty of a wrongdoing. I just knew that person would belittle me with words or even attack me. Belittling a person with stinging words can be just as harsh as physically attacking you. Broken bones will heal, but harsh words can never be retracted and will sting forever.

Our military show great courage. They're ready to give their lives for others. You and I can live in a free country, worship in the church of our choice, go to the schools we select, or vote for who we feel will lead our great nation.

John 16:33 (NASB) tells us, "These things I have spoken to you, that in Me you may have peace. In the world you have tribulation but take courage; I have overcome the world." Jesus says through Him you have courage. All you need to do is ask.

Dear Heavenly Father, I pray each day You lead and guide me through all my trials. Amen.

My Talks with God

INDEPENDENCE

However, in the Lord, neither is woman independent of man, nor is man independent of woman. 1 Corinthians 11:11 (NASB)

A few years ago, I was talking to my brother, and He told me how independent His daughter was. How she wanted to do things on her own. He ended by saying, "She reminds me so much of you. You always struck out on your own, doing things for yourself, never asking for help."

At first, I was upset He made that remark. I'd never thought of myself as being independent, but as years passed, I was reminded of our conversation. As a single parent I felt like I had to fend for myself. I learned how to fix my car, be a plumber, and do anything else that had to be repaired around the house. We had our ups and downs, but we all survived.

Several years later I met and married the love of my life. Since then, I've relinquished some independence. God does have patience. I look to my husband for guidance, but most of all I've learned to depend on God. With prayer and quiet time in His word, my attitude is subdued.

Psalm 119:45 (NASB) tells me I can walk freely with my Lord, but He has also given me the freedom to choose Him or walk the path of worldly ways. I choose my Lord and Savior. I have found peace and comfort.

Gracious Heavenly Father, thank you for the freedom to choose You over the ways of the world. I pray I never walk without you. Amen.

My Talks with God

PROCRASTINATION

Do not boast about tomorrow, for you do not know what a day may bring forth. Proverbs 27:1 (NASB)

Procrastination. Putting off something we really don't want to do or face. Maybe it's not wanting to tell your husband you put a dent in the bumper. He's going to find out sooner or later. Get it out of the way. A sigh of relief. You feel better.

My husband came home the other night and told me a story about a lady who had issues with her pacemaker. Her family finally convinced her to see the doctor. Upon checking, they found a problem with the pacemaker and immediately admitted her. She told her family there's no need to come and sit around. It's a short procedure, in and out in a day. However, something went wrong, and she died on the table. No one waiting. Would family have stood by waiting for news if they had known there was a risk? Did they put it off, thinking it was nothing?

This brings to my mind putting off sharing the Bible with others. There have been times I should have, could have, shared Jesus's love with a friend or stranger, but I did not. I procrastinated.

God doesn't procrastinate, but we do. Because He loves us, He waits for us to come to Him. We are the ones putting off to tomorrow instead of doing today. Don't let another day go by without asking Jesus to come into your heart and take control of your life. Seek His forgiveness.

Dear Heavenly Father, please help me to not put off until tomorrow what I need to do today. Amen.

My Talks with God

MAPS

Set up for yourself road marks, place for yourself guideposts; direct your mind to the highway, the way by which you went. Return, O virgin of Israel, return to these your cities. Jeremiah 31:21 (NASB)

Oh, how I long for a map when I travel. Before the cell phone, my husband bought me a GPS, and I have yet to use it. With a map I can spread it out before me, see all the little roads, major highways, and make my own choices. I may want to take the direct route to get there quicker, that is depending on traffic. Or I may want to take a side road and look at all God has placed in my path to enjoy—the trees, old houses, barns, or maybe even an old broken bridge to nowhere. Hopefully, that broken bridge isn't in my direct path.

If you stop to think about it, our life is much like a map. The path we choose to follow may take us way out of the way. It may take months, or it could be years. Our Heavenly Father gives us the freedom to make our decision.

When we decide to take the long way around, through precarious deep valleys and treacherous high mountains, our Father is waiting for us to call out to Him. In our despair, we fall on our knees and call out for help. He is there and ready. "Here I am. Take my hand and follow me.

Dear Lord, I pray you are always there to give me direction in all I do and say. Amen.

My Talks with God

STARS AND THE HEAVENS

He counts the number of the stars; He gives names to all of them. Psalm 147:4 (NASB)

On any given night you can step outside, look to the sky, and see the stars shining brightly. In junior high I took Astronomy, a chance to study the stars and planets. I'd sit outside with my friends, and we'd try to see if we could pick out the Big Dipper, North Star, Cassiopeia, Pegasus, and Andromeda.

Lovers sit and stare at the stars making wishes. Little children sing "Twinkle, Twinkle Little Star." Some people let the stars guide their lives.

The Bible talks about stars. Revelation 22:16 (NASB) says, "I," Jesus, have sent My angel to testify to you these things for the churches. I am the root and the offspring of David, the bright morning star." Jesus Christ, our Savior, is the Bright Morning Star.

The Twelve Stars in Revelation 12:1 (NASB) represents the twelve tribes of Israel. "And a great sign appeared in heaven: a woman clothed with the sun, and the moon under her feet, and on head a crown of twelve stars." Israel, God's chosen people.

The book of Revelation also talks about the number seven. The seven stars, seven lamp stands, seven angels who had seven plagues, and the seven Spirits of God that are all warnings from God telling us of the end times.

After studying the book of Revelation, I have a new insight when I look upward. Each star has a new meaning.

Father, thank you for Your word and each beautiful star that shines at night. Your way of telling me, "I love you. Here is another gift for you." Amen.

My Talks with God

PRAISE

And the heavens will praise Thy wonders, O Lord: Thy faithfulness also in the assembly of the holy ones. Psalm 89:5 (NASB)

Today like every day I want to praise my Lord. Usually, I open my prayer with I praise you, Lord, for all you do daily in my life. But today I felt like I wanted to take it a step further.

HE IS

HE IS the sun and moon

the bright evening star.

HE IS the thunder and lightning

the mighty hurricane, tornado, and earthquake.

HE IS a newborn's cry

the gentle touch of a hand.

He IS the fragrance of a new rose

the fresh smell of summer rain.

HE IS the roar of the lion

the sting of a bee, the bite of a snake.

HE IS the air you breathe

the wind in the trees,

the sound of a fast-moving stream.

Be silent and listen.

HE IS.

Gracious Heavenly Father, thank you for every breath I take, for my sight, feeling, and for every new day You give me, and for all You do in my life. Amen.

My Talks with God

BOOMPA

Grandchildren are the crowning glory of the aged; parents are the pride of their children. Proverbs 17:6 (NLT)

My husband and I were visiting his aunt Eleanor in Missouri after her husband's death. I could sit for hours and listen to her Irish brogue as she told stories of their life together. She liked telling stories about her husband, George, and one night before turning in she said, "I've a story to tell you about George and how he became known as 'Boompa'."

When their daughter found out she was pregnant, she announced to her mother, "I want Dad's grandchildren to call him Boompa." Eleanor said she fumbled for words. Whoever heard of a grandfather being called Boompa? That's a silly name.

Nevertheless, when their first grandchild was old enough, he began calling George, Boompa. As the years rolled on, each grandchild after that called him Boompa, too.

When their grandson graduated from high school, he walked out on stage, received his diploma, then turned around with his diploma held over his head, and yelled, "For you Boompa."

There were giggles throughout the auditorium, but when Eleanor looked at George's face, he was smiling from ear to ear. She said, "I guess that wasn't such a bad name for him after all."

Our Heavenly Father loves us even more than we love our children and grandchildren. He loves it when we call Him Abba, Jehovah, El Shaddai, El Elyon, Elohim, El Olam, Immanuel, Yahweh, or Adonai. These names are endearing to His ears.

Dear Father, I thank you for all the blessings you bestow upon me and my loved ones. I bow down before you. Thank you El Elyon, Amen.

My Talks with God

MOTHER'S SWEATER

I am with you always, to the end of the age. Matthew 28:20 (NASB)

My mother lived in Seattle during the eighties, and my family lived in Texas. In July or August, I would take a couple of weeks and go visit her. Summers are quite different between the two states. Invariably, I would go without something to keep me warm during the chilly evenings when we sat on the patio talking. Mom would say, "Honey, go get one of my sweaters."

In the back of my mind, I think I left my sweaters at home purposely, because when I picked out one of hers, I would slide my arm slowly in one sleeve then into the other. I smelled her fragrance left behind. It filled my senses while wrapping my arms around myself remembering how she comforted me when I cried or just felt down in the dumps over something going on in my life. I felt secure in her arms.

As I've grown in my life as a Christian, I've come to feel the presence of Jesus much like the times I wore my mother's sweater. At times I'd plunge along each day without praying, then my life seemed like it went out of control. I knew it was time to pray and get back on track with my Lord. I felt His loving arms wrapped around me comforting me, filling me with His warmth. I felt secure again knowing I don't have to go through this life alone. He is always with me.

Thank you, Lord, for never leaving me even when I think I can handle everything by myself. Amen

My Talks with God

BUSYBODIES

We hear that some among you are leading an undisciplined life, doing no work at all, but acting like busybodies. Now such persons we command and exhort in the Lord Jesus Christ to work in quiet fashion and eat their own bread. II Thessalonians 3:11-12 (NASB)

This may seem an odd scripture for today, but after talking with a friend, I thought this may be a good time to address the life of a busybody. My friend proceeded to tell me of her mother-in-law and her daughter. Both had been gossiping about each other. They didn't want to be in the same house together. The mother-in-law went so far as to say, "Please don't let my daughter be at my funeral." How sad that their lives grew apart so much that they could not and would not be referred to in the same sentence.

Hearing this brought back memories of overhearing a friend repeat gossip she'd heard about me. I asked where she had heard such a thing. After much hesitation, she told me. I was heartbroken when she said it was my best friend of fifteen years. We'd gone to high school together and had been witnesses for each other when we married.

I prayed for God to guard my tongue before I confronted my friend. Her curt reply was, "I just repeated what I'd heard." I finally said, "Because of our friendship you should have come to me."

Where and how does gossip start? A misspoken word taken in the wrong context or perhaps something in your own life is not going right, and it's easier to blame others. Whatever the reason, we are to seek God's guidance before we speak. We are to lift each other up.

Dear Heavenly Father, I pray for your guidance in guarding my tongue when I speak to others and to lift them up in prayer. Amen.

My Talks with God

SHE LOVED ME STILL

Even before He made the world, God loved us and chose us in Christ to be holy and without fault in His eyes. Ephesians 1:4 (NLT)

After writing a scathing letter to my mother, I felt all pious and self-righteous. After all, she was wrong, or so I thought. We lived quite a distance from each other, phone calls were costly at the time, and I was a young mother of three myself; hence, the letter.

Time passed, I grew up, moved about due to military moves, and then ended up living with my mother when I returned from Germany. I'd forgotten about the letter. My life was not going so well. Mom never mentioned the letter.

It wasn't until I'd been living on my own again that I was feeling melancholy thinking about my past and how I ended up on my own with one child still at home. I began thinking about my mother's life and how she wound up on her own, all six children gone. The memory of the letter hit me right smack in the face. How could I have sent her that awful letter. It must have hurt her to the core. All in all, many years had passed, and she never mentioned it. I was too ashamed to say anything. But she loved me enough to not say a word.

Then I recalled how much God loves me. When I became a Christian, confessed my sins, and professed my love for him, He wiped away all my sins. I am His. A mother's love is great, but God's love is even greater.

Dear Father in heaven thank you for loving me so much you wiped away all my sins. I am yours forever.

My Talks with God

PAIN

"Is it nothing to all you who pass this way? Look and see if there is any pain like my pain which was severely delt out to me. Which the Lord inflicted on the day of His fierce anger.
Lamentations 1:12 (NASB)

Television ads display aspirin and all other pain remedies every fifteen minutes on some channel. For arthritis, migraines, and just about any other ailment, there is the old saying, "Take this pill and call me in the morning if the pain hasn't gone away."

I remember sitting next to my mother and watching tears roll down her cheeks. When I asked her if she was alright, her reply was, "Oh, honey, the pain is so bad it hurts to move." She had osteoarthritis. Her once long, beautiful, fingers were now crippled to the point she could no longer wear her rings. Her toes were bent to where she couldn't wear shoes, but she padded along in her house slippers everywhere.

Since my seventieth birthday, I have suffered from arthritis along with my brother, who has had it since fifty. I hobble now when I walk unlike the spry gait I once had in my twenties.

When I start to complain about my pain, I've had to stop myself. My Jesus suffered much more pain on the cross than I could have ever endured. He did it for me and for you. He took my sin on His shoulders so I could spend eternity with him. By God's grace I am saved through the blood of Jesus Christ.

Merciful Father, I thank you for your Son Jesus who died for my sins. Forgive me for complaining about my small aches and pains. They are nothing like the pain You suffered for me. Amen.

My Talks with God

ACQUIRE WISDOM

Acquire wisdom! Acquire understanding! Do not forget, nor turn away from the words of my mouth. Proverbs 4:5 (NASB)

This morning while my daughter and I were at the pool for our workout, we were reflecting on years ago when she visited her brother during the summer. Then the subject turned to one of her sisters and asked why I didn't stop her when she moved out at thirteen. "Mom did you kick her out or did she move out? I was too young to remember."

How do you tell your daughter at some point you have to let go? I began. "If I'd tried to stop her, she would have run away. I might not have ever seen her again. If I let her go, I could keep an eye on her and watch her as she went about. I didn't agree with her lifestyle, but in my heart, I knew she would come home. It took six months for her to realize she'd made a mistake, and I know it had to be hard for her to admit she was wrong and move back home."

Like so many parents, we want to shield our children of the hurts and misfortunes that we endured. It's hard when you must let go so they can make their own mistakes.

I am thankful that my Lord let me go through the calamities I did to acquire the wisdom He wanted me to have. At times I felt all alone with no one to turn to. No one to talk to and comfort me. When I was at my lowest point, God was with me. He held me in His hands and shielded me from harm. We can only pray that He is with our children as they go out into the world to find their own wisdom.

Gracious Heavenly Father, watch over my children, shield and protect them as they leave and find their way in life. Amen.

My Talks with God

CHILDREN

Jesus said, "Let the children alone, and do not hinder them from coming to me; for the kingdom of heaven belongs to such as these." Matthew 19:14 (NASB)

Pick up a newspaper, magazine, or turn on the television and you see shootings, stabbings, beatings of children. Yes, children. It's one thing for adults to get upset with another adult and take their anger out physically. When they lash out at a child, that is another thing.

A helpless child looks up to their elders for guidance. From early childhood, children learn from grown-ups how to talk, walk, run, and play. When children see adults fight and curse, they, in turn, do the same. They see it on television and in movies.

My heart is heavy for each one of these children and my own grandchildren who have witnessed ugly divorces where the parents use name-calling and even physical abuse.

Statistics will tell you children usually repeat what they see or been brought up around. Today I ask you to take time to pray for children, whether you know them or not, that God watch over them and deliver them from this environment.

Gracious Lord, I pray for every child on earth that there is someone close to them that will tell them, or be an example to them, that your love is forever. Let them know they are a child of yours. Amen.

My Talks with God

APPROVAL

For He who in this way serves Christ is acceptable to God and approved by men. Romans 14:18 (NASB)

When my girls were in high school, they always dressed to look good for the boys and show off to the other girls the latest new clothes and fashion. Although they wouldn't admit it, they were looking for approval from their peers.

I've seen neighbors go out and buy the newest lawnmowers, edgers, and barbecues to show off. Whether they bought the gadgets because they really needed them or perhaps theirs had worn out. If we were to think about it, they too are likely looking for approval from others.

Approval comes in many different forms. There's getting accepted into the most prestigious school, making the football team, cheerleading squad, or getting on a swim team. Children do things to please their parents to get their approval. Adults will do the same.

In our world today with people looking the other way, a strong man who has faith in the Lord will live His life for God. This man is acceptable in God's eyes and an example to other men.

Dear Lord, I pray for all the Godly men, that they are an example for others to follow. Amen.

My Talks with God

DARKNESS

He brought them out of darkness and the shadow of death and broke their bands apart. Psalms 107:14 (NASB)

A few days ago, I was talking to a friend. She told me about a friend of hers that was going through a period of darkness in her life. Her husband had been in Iraq and upon his return, she said he had changed. They started having marital problems and separated.

My grandson also was in Iraq. He was only nineteen when he was sent over there. Upon his return, his marriage fell apart and he found himself divorced. He was living in deep darkness.

We cannot fathom what our men go through, what they see, or how they feel during the throes of war. The suffering, turmoil, and stress of everyday dodging bullets, bombs, or watching their comrades fall before their eyes.

War is something that can't be fixed overnight with so many hindrances to overcome. This can put some people into deep despair, leading into an even deeper darkness. Some have even taken their lives, because they've fallen so far into a dark hole they didn't know how to get out.

This darkness is not only for men at war, but for anyone going through a divorce, losing a loved one, or even being in an accident. I felt the darkness while going through a divorce but was renewed through God's love. In my darkest hour I reached for my Bible and started reading. His words comforted me, and I felt restored. Even now when I feel down and not able to fix a situation, my Bible is opened to where God is leading.

Father God I pray for everyone that is going through a rough period in their life. A period that has overshadowed their lives and flung them into darkness. May your Word lift them up into the light. Amen.

My Talks with God

GENEALOGY

Without father, without mother, without genealogy, having neither beginning of days nor end of life, but made like the Son of God, He abides a priest perpetually. Hebrews 7:3 (NASB)

Last night I went to a genealogy group that just formed at our library. Since genealogy is my passion, I wanted to know if someone else found a better website or a new way to find that elusive relative. Some people had been tracing their lineage for quite a few years and some were beginners. One gentleman said he had his DNA tested but wasn't sure if it's helped him or not. He was still having trouble figuring out the markers, etc. I told him I had my DNA tested also, and I too, was confused on where I was in the big picture.

It's exciting when you find that relative you've been searching for. You want to shout it out to everyone. I've caught myself sitting at the computer throwing my hands in the air and shouting, "I found him!"

Think of how much more God is excited when another child of His has accepted His grace and life everlasting. That thought is beyond my wildest dreams. I cannot grasp His jubilant reaction, or the sweet and pure sound of His angels singing.

Gracious Heavenly Father, thank you for the love You've given me just for being Your child. Amen.

My Talks with God

WORLDLY TREASURES

For every beast of the forest is Mine, the cattle on a thousand hills. Psalms 50:10 (NASB)

Eighteen years ago, I had the opportunity to see Lulu Roman at a church concert. Lulu Roman graced the stage on the old television program "Hee-Haw." Occasionally she was asked to sing gospel music. Her full, rich, voice caressed each word when she praised God. After sharing her testimony, she sang a song she wrote, "Shopping List." I was so impressed with the words; I bought the cassette and played it repeatedly until I was able to write all the words down. I keep it in my address book and read it from time to time to remind me that all my worldly treasures are only mine for a little while; they belong to my Heavenly Father. He loves me so much He gives these treasures to me to enjoy in my earthly life.

She sings about praying, about God's mercy and love, then on to all the gimme things she thinks are important in her life. Lulu paints a picture in words of how we ask God for the things we think are what we need to make us happy. We forget that all we have belongs to God. From the cattle on a thousand hills to the tiny hummingbird perched on the feeder outside my window. We can build a fortune here on earth but in the end, we cannot take it with us when we pass on. It is God's gift to us, but what we do with it is our responsibility. To share God's gift with others should be our aspiration.

Heavenly Father, I pray I never take advantage of all You do for me. Just to wake up each day and breathe the fresh air, to hear the birds sing, or see the trees sway in the breeze. Thank you, Lord. Amen.

My Talks with God

GROWING OLD SHOULDN'T HURT

"For I will restore you to health and I will heal you of your wounds," declares the Lord. Jeremiah 30:17 (NASB)

I awoke early one morning ready to get all the things done that I had to do. But before I could put my feet on the floor my stomach gave a lurch, and my head pounded. No, I cried, not today. I have so much to take care of. I laid my head down and closed my eyes. An hour later I opened one eye and looked at the clock. Seven. I have to get up; the dogs need to be fed. Every joint in my body resisted as I made my way into the kitchen. I called my girlfriend and told her I wouldn't make it to breakfast that morning. After feeding and bringing the dogs back in, I grabbed my blanket and headed for the couch.

By ten I convinced myself no matter how bad I felt, I needed to get up and get going. I headed to the pharmacy to refill my prescriptions. Every step I took was excruciating. My knees didn't want to cooperate, and my head still throbbed. I began wondering *where did this come from*?

I've always prided myself with being able to take care of everyone else. I take my vitamins each morning along with my prescribed medications. My lazy Susan is full of every vitamin you can think of to keep me healthy.

Before dinner I went in and checked my e-mail and noticed my Bible laying under some of the things I was working on. I'm not very tidy when I'm working on a project. Things get stacked on top of each other. Seeing the Bible reminded me to stop and think of how my body was going to feel when I'm taken home to live with my Savior for eternity. Praise God there will be no more pain. I'm not a runner but I'll bet I'll be able to run. Maybe even skip like I did as a child. God gave you and me that promise when He said He will restore our health.

Dear Father in Heaven, thank you for always keeping your promises. Amen.

My Talks with God

BITTERNESS

Let all bitterness and wrath and anger and clamor and slander be put away from you, along with all malice. Ephesians 4:31 (NASB)

Recently, I chatted with a friend about her family. I asked how her father was doing these days and she replied, "Please do not speak his name around me ever again." I was surprised at her comment and asked why she felt that way. Surely it couldn't be that bad. She went on to tell me about the lies, name calling, and gossip he was spreading about her and her family.

Later I spoke with her brother, and he told me the same story but added a bit more of which I wasn't aware. She was still holding a grudge against her father for giving her up when she was a teenager. It seems when her parents divorced and her mother remarried, her father gave her up for adoption. She still carries that scar and has let it fester over the years.

When I heard that, I called and spoke to her about not letting the bitterness take over her life. I knew that allowing this to take control would end up taking her down to the lowest abyss possible. When that happens, your health goes astray and you start to doubt everyone around you. I prayed with her. Now it is up to her to give it over to the Lord and let Him be the guide in her life.

No matter what someone else has done to you, it is far better to let God take control than let it destroy your life. This is hard because we are only human, and our first response is to get even or wish something bad on that individual.

Dear Heavenly Father, I lift my friend up to you and pray she finds peace and lets go of all bitterness against her father. To let You handle her life. You know what is best for us. Amen.

My Talks with God

COMFORT

Great is my confidence in you, great is my boasting on your behalf; I am filled with comfort. I am overflowing with joy in all your affliction. II Corinthians 7:4 NAS

It's been a few years since my youngest brother passed away. He fought the good fight until the colon cancer became too much and overtook his weakened body. I sat by his side for a week while we celebrated his life. We set off fireworks observing the 4th of July, fixed his favorite meals, and talked about old times. I arrived home on Monday and the Lord took him home on Tuesday.

During the time of my brother's cancer my sister-in-law developed breast cancer. They both went through chemo and radiation together. She laid him to rest and just one year later her cancer returned. She went through the regimen again. Her hair fell out but grew back very curly and gray. We joked about her curly hair and turning gray before me, since I am ten years older than either of them. Not long after finding out her cancer was in remission she was diagnosed with pancreatic cancer. She refused treatment saying it was more than she could bear.

I tell you this story because their family's love for Christ has sustained them throughout their lives. It's hard to lose a loved one. But when these family members are left behind, they know they will see their loved ones again, and that's reassuring and sustains them each day. He gives them strength to go on. Our God comforts us in our times of loss and despair.

Praise God. Gracious Father, I pray you comfort the families during their time of loss. Keep them in Your gentle hands and guide them each day. Amen.

My Talks with God

THE FINEST

Bring the finest robe in the house and put it on him. Get a ring for His finger and sandals for His feet. Luke 15:22 NLT

When we go out for a job interview, we put our best foot forward so to speak. We make sure our clothes are cleaned and pressed, shoes shined, and our hair is in place. Think about the first date you went on. You wanted to make an impression, so you picked out the best restaurant, cleaned your car, and made sure your clothes were in tip top shape. No loose strings, stains, or tears. You might have even gone out and bought new clothes.

Aunt Hazel came for a visit, and we put out the best China, cleaned the house, and made her favorite dish for dinner. You might want to call this putting on airs, but don't you want to give her the best we have?

How much more are we to give to our Lord? Do we not owe Him our best? Like my mother used to say, "Don't do the job halfway, go the extra mile, and do your best."

When the Lord asks us to do something we should give Him our best. Think of how your earthly father is gladdened in what you do then magnify it one hundred times over. That is how God delights in you giving your best.

Gracious Heavenly Father, I pray I do my best in all I do for You. I want to glorify You. Amen.

My Talks with God

BELIEVE

You can pray for anything, and if you have faith, you will receive it.
Matthew 21:22 NLT

Believe…this is a hard one. I believe and I have faith, but do I have enough faith to believe in what I ask for will be given? This morning as I was mulling over what I wanted to write about, or what God wanted me to write about, the word "believe" kept coming to mind. I believe in myself, that I can do anything I set my mind to. I believe if I touch a hot stove, I'm going to get burnt. I believe that if I keep writing, I will become proficient in making my sentences speak with meaning and put the punctation marks in the right places.

Many years ago, when I was going through a rough time my prayers to God were, *if you do this for me, and I believed it would happen, then I would do that for You.* I couldn't understand why my prayers weren't answered. I believed and I had faith. As I grew in my knowledge of the Lord, I understood why He didn't answer my prayers the way I wanted Him to. Like an earthly father, our Heavenly Father knows what is best for us. We have to believe in His wisdom and His timing for our prayers to be answered, and in His way. How much better are His ways than ours! Like a spoiled child I wanted things my way, and I wanted them then, not later. Now in my later years God has blessed me more than a hundred times over. Something I would never have seen years ago.

Heavenly Father, please be patient with me when I pray for things. I believe they will be answered, but they will be answered according to Your will and not mine. Amen.

My Talks with God

MEANINGLESS

But pity the man who falls and has no one to help Him up.
Ecclesiastes 4:10 (NIV)

I've been reading Ecclesiastes, and it has made me take a hard look at my life, a hard look at me. The me that will go out and buy a new blouse to make me feel good or because nothing in my closet fits just right this morning. The me that needs one more thing in my sewing room, because I couldn't find what I was looking for to begin with. All this stuff is meaningless. When I die, there won't be a luggage rack on the top of the hearse taking my body to the cemetery. I cannot stuff goodies in the casket with me hoping to use later.

What I need to be looking at is, what have I done in my life—not the things or stuff I have in my life. Did I take the time to talk to my neighbor instead of waving to them when they pulled out of the driveway this morning? Did I listen to my children when they tried to get my attention wanting to talk? Did I brush them off and say later, perhaps when I have more time?

For the homeless, have I helped serve them a meal, speak to them about Jesus, give them a blanket to keep them warm, or just sit and listen to them talk? The widows in the nursing home, did I take time to brush their hair, hold their hand when they were feeling alone, or read to them because their eyes were failing? Ecclesiastes has opened my eyes.

Dear Father, thank you for opening my eyes. Forgive me for my short comings, and I pray for Your help to be the person You want me to be. Amen.

My Talks with God

GOD TALKING

And the foundations of the thresholds trembled at the voice of Him who called out. Isaiah 6:4 (NAS)

When my granddaughter visited me, she told me she took her three-year-old daughter to Vacation Bible School at a Catholic Church this summer. One day she was early, so she slipped inside the door while they prayed. She tried to be quiet, but her daughter looked up and saw her. She said, “Mom, it’s God. God’s talking.”

Out of the mouths of babes. Or is it? Have you stopped to think about God talking to you? I’d like to think that when I get a certain tugging on my heart, my mind, or whatever you want to call it, it’s God talking to me. You might even say it’s your conscience.

God is gentle, kind, all knowing, loving, merciful, and mighty. When He speaks, mountains bow down, thunder rolls, lightning cracks across the sky. Foundation’s tremble and oceans pound the surf.

God speaks to each one of us differently. Stop and listen. He may appear in your dreams, whisper in your ear, or tug at your heart. Your inner being. He wants and waits to talk to you.

Abba Father, thank you for wanting to talk to me, your daughter. I wait in anticipation for your soft nudging. Amen.

My Talks with God

MY SAUCER IS FULL

Now you have every spiritual gift you need as you eagerly wait for the return of our Lord Jesus Christ. 1 Corinthians 1:7 (NLT)

I read a poem once titled 'My Cup Has Overflowed' by John Paul Moore. It made me stop and think about my life and how much God blesses me. I couldn't say it any better than this.

John's poem says:

> I've never made a fortune, and it's probably too late now. But I don't worry about that much, I'm happy anyhow.
>
> And as I go along life's way, I'm reaping better than I sowed. I'm drinking from my saucer, 'cause my cup has overflowed.

There are four more stanzas to the poem, and He ends it by saying:

> Then I'll keep drinking from my saucer,
>
> cause my cup has overflowed."

When I'm feeling down, I remember this poem and chastise myself. I'm reminded of all the things my Savior has done for me. I can never thank Him enough for the many blessings He has given me.

Precious Jesus, thank you for all you've done for me. May I never forget how much you love me and all you do in my life, and I will continue to drink from my saucer. Amen.

My Talks with God

MAN'S BREATH

For they are like a breath of air; their days are like a passing shadow. Psalms 144:4 (NLT)

I read this verse a few days ago and wrote it down. It has plagued me each day as I sit at my computer. I've dismissed it, but somehow it keeps looming back up.

Each day passes by so fast I cannot even begin to get all the things done that I want to do. By the end of the day, I've gotten upset with myself because I did not write any new pages for my novel. With this snail crawl, I'll never get it finished.

Oh, I get up early enough, but then it's "take care of this," "take care of that," laundry, dusting, vacuuming, running errands. Then it's time to fix dinner and spend time with hubby.

Growing up, each day seemed to linger. I could lie in the grass and watch the clouds float across the sky. Skip rocks on the pond, ride my bike, skip a rope and maybe read a book. Life dragged on each day. I looked forward to my birthday, Christmas, and summer vacation with great anticipation.

Looking back, I wonder where did all those days, weeks, months, and years go? I'm in the autumn of my life. My life went by too fast. Yes, I still have a lot of years left but the growing up, marriage, raising children seems like a blur, like a fleeting shadow.

My life has been blessed because I'm a child of God. He has given me strength each day. My Fortress in whom I trust. He gave me salvation when I asked Him for forgiveness of my sins. He is my all in all.

Dear Father in heaven, thank you for taking care of me all my life. Thank you for being my strength daily and my fortress when I was in despair. Amen.

My Talks with God

BREATHLESS

God called the dry ground "land" and the waters "seas" and God saw that it was good. Genesis 1:10 (NLT)

It's that time of the year we go hustling and bustling around to do everything at once. Shopping, cleaning, Christmas cards, and the lists go on. We find ourselves running so fast it leaves us breathless.

Breathless…it brought other thoughts to mind. I went camping with a friend many years ago to Nelson, British Columbia. As we drove through the mountains, I leaned my head back against the seat and marveled at the sight. It seemed like the mountains reached the heavens. Majestic, standing so tall, covered with pine trees. It was, in a sense, breathless.

My mother and I took a trip along the Washington coast one day. We stopped and got out of the car at one of the roadside rests. Driftwood dotted the beach. The ocean looked like glass in the distance as small waves rolled on shore. Silence except for the waves. A picture of tranquility. Breathless.

Still on another trip to Ruidoso, New Mexico, my husband and I sat on the front porch of our cabin and listened as the wind blew through the tall pines. Occasionally a squirrel scurried from tree to tree. It was so quiet except for a bird now and then calling for His mate. Breathless.

My thoughts went to Mary and Joseph when Jesus was born. Holding her tiny baby in her arms and knowing He was God's son. She must have felt breathless.

I feel breathless at times knowing I am a child of God. By grace through faith, I am saved. Breathless.

Dear Father, thank you for Your precious son, Jesus, who was born and then died for my sins. Thank you for your sacrifice. I am breathless. Amen.

My Talks with God

THE BIG BANG

Then God said, "Let lights appear in the sky to separate the day from the night." Genesis l:14 (NLT)

It's that time of the year again. Holidays and more holidays. It starts with harvest festivals, Thanksgiving, Christmas, and then New Years. One big party after another. The scurrying here and there, buying gifts, decorating, and it goes on and on.

I think it's time we slow down and reflect on the true meaning of the holidays. In the beginning, there was God and God alone. He created the earth, stars, planets, moon, trees, lakes, oceans, and whew, man and woman!

To complete His work He promised a savior, the Messiah. The Messiah, Jesus, will come to save each one of us from our sin. That we must keep vigil and watch for His coming.

I think at times I've been caught up in the hype of ads in the media, and the stores wanting to get the jump on the holidays. We've pushed aside the true meaning of the holidays.

Harvest festival was a time of getting together after the farmers brought their crops in. Work had been completed; they were ready for the winter. The pilgrims were grateful to God for seeing them through their first winter in America. They celebrated together with the friendly Indians and a feast.

Christmas, Christ's birth. Fulfilling the promise God made to His people. The Messiah. The virgin birth of His son who came to earth, died on the cross, and rose again to save us all.

And then there is the New Year. A new beginning. A time to make promises to yourself and others on how you are going to make this next year a better one.

All of this means that God gave us our beautiful world to live in. The stars, moon, trees, flowers, and most of all His Son. A promise that He would return and take His children to reign on high with Him. Praise God.

Thank you, Lord, for all the stars in the heavens, the moon and planets to marvel at when I look into the sky. But most of all thank you for your Son, Jesus, who died for me. Thank you. Amen.

My Talks with God

HIS TIME IS NEAR

Listen! My beloved! Behold, He is coming, climbing on the mountains, leaping on the hills! Song of Solomon 2:8 (NAS)

I opened my Bible this morning and this is what jumped out. At one time I highlighted this verse. The book of Solomon is a love song depicting the wooing and wedding of a shepherdess. But it also illustrates Israel as God's bride and the Church as the bride of Christ.

As I read it, I thought of what was going on in the world today. Listen—everyone who can hear. God is calling you to take heed. Listen to your heart as He speaks to you. Listen to the warnings that are written in His Word of what will happen before Jesus' return.

My Beloved. You are His beloved. He created you. He wants to have fellowship with you. He loves you, pure and simple. It doesn't get any plainer than this.

Behold, He is coming. It is written in His Word Jesus was born, died on the cross, arose and will come again to take His children home. Home to reign with Him on high.

Climbing on the mountains. He is waiting for you to accept Him. He knocks, speaks to your heart, and waits for you to respond. Do not wait too long.

Leaping on the hills. He rejoices and the angels sing with resounding song when you accept His love. He waits with great anticipation to be able to talk with you, to sing with you, and to guide you throughout your daily journey. Let Him direct you. You cannot do it alone. He never wanted you to do it on your own. He is your Shield, Protector and Comforter.

Heavenly Father, I come to you today and ask you to guide each one of us as we go through the day. Keep our eyes on You. I pray this in Jesus' name. Amen.

My Talks with God

I HAVE A DREAM

As for these four youths, God gave them knowledge and intelligence in every branch of literature and wisdom. Daniel 1:17 (NAS)

We all dream; some dreams are more real than others. Most of our dreams we forget as soon as we wakeup. But then there are the ones that we remember and can't shake or get out of our minds.

I had one such dream. I'd been to a writers' conference and when I returned home, I was all pumped up and ready to write. One conference leader spoke right to me. I know she did; it was like she'd been hiding in my house watching me. I tucked away all the information that seeped into my brain and walked around with tiny bits vying for attention. I went to bed thinking of all this stuff. During the night I dreamed I received a check for five thousand dollars for a book I wrote. You can imagine how I felt the next morning. *I got money for a story I wrote! I need to work on that story and finish it.*

Now, the book is finished and published. Although it hasn't made me rich as far as money is deemed, I am by far richer than I could ever imagine. I've made so many friends along the way. I've traveled to places I only dreamed about to find out more of the pieces of my life and discovered the hidden parts of my life I knew nothing of. I am much richer than gold.

I believe my story and the check I dreamed about is God's way of telling me I have great things planned for you. Follow me, I will never leave you. I will guide you. Keep your eyes upon Me.

Gracious Heavenly Father, thank you for never leaving me and making me richer than I could ever have imagined.

My Talks with God

NO WORRIES

Don't worry about tomorrow, for tomorrow will bring its own worries. Today's trouble is enough for today. Matthew 6:34 (NLT)

There have been times I'd begin to worry about one thing then another. Things like when we had to buy a new set of tires and there really wasn't enough money in the savings; or when we received a higher electric bill than what I'd budgeted for. I'd even wake up in the middle of the night and start to think of what I had been thinking of during the day. Then I couldn't get back to sleep.

Our Father says give that worry to Him and He will take care of it. All I know is when I give it to Him, I feel at peace knowing He is in control. Matthew 6:9-13 says it so much better:

Our Father in heaven, may your name be kept holy.

May your will be done on earth as it is in heaven.

Give us today the food we need, and forgive us our sins, as we have forgiven those who sin against us.

And don't let us yield to temptation but rescue us from the evil one.

Those worries will always be there, but it's so much easier when I give them over to my heavenly Father to take care of than when I sit and worry over how *I* was going to take care of it.

Dear Father, thank you for always being with me where I can come to you and let you know what is on my mind. You always know before I do what is going to happen and are waiting for me. I pray I never forget that. Amen.

My Talks with God

RUNNING AWAY

We do not know what we ought to pray for, but the Spirit himself intercedes for us with groans that words cannot express.
Romans 8:26 (NIV)

I've always considered myself shy. I never raised my hand in class, even if I knew the answer to the question. I didn't want to draw attention to myself. I liked sitting in the back of the room no matter where I went.

I took speech in my junior year and when it was my turn to get up in front of the class my hands felt sweaty. I wobbled down the aisle to the front of everyone. I felt flushed and was sure my face was fiery red. When I turned around and looked into each face staring back at me, my knees felt like rubber. All that was audible were small squeaks and whispers as I tried to speak. I swallowed the lump in my throat and told the joke I heard my mother tell my father a few nights ago and when I was finished, I ran back to my chair and sat down. No one laughed, in fact no one said anything. I never wanted to do that again.

When it was time for me to find a summer job, I made my girlfriend go with me to all the stores to fill out the applications. I was terrified I would say the wrong thing and get laughed at.

I'm not going to say I outgrew being shy because I still would rather sit in the back of the room. The only thing different now is that I have Someone I can turn to for strength and support. He never leaves me.

He is my Savior Christ Jesus. Even though I gave my life to Him when I was sixteen, I continued to do my own thing. Oh, I said my prayers, gave thanks at meals, and went through the motions. Not until I went through a nasty divorce did I realize how much strength

I had in Him and how many times Jesus held me in His arms keeping me safe. I felt peace.

Even though Jesus is in my life, every day is a struggle. The evil one never leaves me alone. The only difference now is that through Jesus I can fight the temptations that come my way.

Dear Heavenly Father, thank you for your son, Jesus, who never leaves me. Thank you for giving me the strength I need each day. Amen.

My Talks with God

HOME SWEET HOME

For man goes to His eternal home while mourners go about in the street. Ecclesiastes 12:5 (NIV)

While shopping at a craft store, my friend and I came across homemade signs saying, "Home Sweet Home" and "Home Is Where the Heart Is." There were other cutesy signs with similar sayings leaving one to believe home is where one can feel safe and loved.

In these troubled times, not every home is safe nor does everyone feel loved. Home can be a lonely place, a place of violence, or alcohol abuse. Children come home every day to an empty home because both parents work, and they cannot afford a sitter. So, the child lets himself in and sits in front of the television, does his homework, or plays computer games.

Perhaps the child goes home to parents that are out of work, angry with each other, then taking it out on the child, or even each other. Angry words are said in haste. Hurting words once said can never be retracted. The child retreats to his room and closes the door sitting in silence.

There are trials in each of our lives. It's how we react to those trials that make us a stronger person. Without God's guidance and love, we cannot face the adversity that the evil one throws our way.

I know when my life feels out of control and Satan is attacking me or my family, I go straight away to God in prayer. When I am through voicing my concerns, I feel a peace about me. I may know my situation isn't going to change, but I also know with God I can handle whatever comes my way. He is my voice and strength.

Most Gracious Father, I thank you for never leaving me. You are my Rock, and Substance. Be with me in tough times and good. Amen.

My Talks with God

TREASURES

"They will be mine," says the Lord Almighty," in the day when I prepare my treasured possession and I will spare them, just as in compassion a man spares His son, who serves him."
Malachi 3:17 (NIV)

My family has watched "National Treasure" about six times now. Each time we get just as excited as the first time when they find the buried treasure. Then, there are the pirate movies searching for ships to plunder and send to the bottom of the ocean. Everyone is searching for treasure to become wealthy.

I have certain things my mother and grandmother gave me long ago I consider my treasures. They are precious to me because they were given by loved ones.

God says we are His treasures. He made us, knows us inside out, and loves us unconditionally. He longs for quiet fellowship with us. He wants to hear what is troubling us, our longings, and fears. Just like your earthly father, God desires companionship with you.

Our earthly treasures are trivial, but God's treasures are priceless. We are valued and precious in His sight. All He asks of us is to confess our sins to Him and let Him come into our heart to forever follow Him. He will give us eternal life. A life everlasting in His heavenly home.

Dear Heavenly Father, thank you for letting me be your treasurer. Amen.

My Talks with God

CAN WE TALK?

Stop depriving one another, except by mutual consent and for a time that you may devote yourselves to prayer. Then come together again so that Satan will not tempt you because of your lack of self-control.
I Corinthians 7:5 (NIV)

There are days when I feel the need to borrow the phrase from Joan Rivers, "Can we talk?" I have to make myself take the time to sit down and have a heart-to-heart with God. The busyness of the day grips me and it is evening before I realize I didn't take time to commune with my Lord.

Like most of us I go throughout the day and talk with God. You know what I mean. "Lord, don't let that driver pull out in front of me." Or "Lord, give me one more minute to finish this and I'll sit down with you."

He wants His time with me. Me alone. My complete self, not just a passing moment to say a prayer, which I might add, becomes automatic sometimes. Again, you know what I'm saying. "Lead me through this day, watch over my children, guide my husband in His decisions; and oh, yes, Lord, we need rain. Amen."

No, God wants me to take TIME for Him. To open my Bible and let Him lead me in scripture. What He's saying to me and me alone. He already knows my heart, but He wants me to talk to Him like I would to my closest friend.

Do you not love your own children and want the best for them? God is our Father and He wants what is best for us.

Matthew 21:22 (NIV) says If you believe, you will receive whatever you ask for in prayer. This doesn't mean we need to ask to win the lottery. What it does mean is God wants us to live a full and abundant life, and above all, take time for Him.

Dear Heavenly Father, thank you for Your love and always being there for me. Forgive me for not taking time to be with You. I need You in my life as I cannot do anything without You. Amen.

My Talks with God

WHO AM I?

Being then the offspring of God, we ought not to think that the Divine Nature is like gold or silver or stone, an image formed by the art and thought of man. Acts 17:29 (NAS)

WHO am I?…Who *AM* I?…Who am *I*? It's all on the emphasis. Cecil Murphy asked the same questions in his December newsletter. I had been thinking along this line for quite some time myself. Sorry, Cec, I need to add answers.

I am a wife, a mother, sister, aunt, grandmother, daughter, and I am also me. The me who is asking the question. Yes, I know I am a child of God, His daughter, and that He loves me, but who am I? I believe most people have asked themselves the same question at some point.

Wife—I am the one who lifts my husband up to God every day in prayer. Stands by His side when He is sick and rejoices when He is well. Keeps His home comfortable, cooks His meals, runs His errands, and soothes His brow.

Mother—I lift my children in prayer every day, kiss the boo boo's, play dolls or ball with them, drive them to games, dances, movies, or friends' homes. I'm there to listen when they are hurting or share their victories. Guide them with their choices.

Daughter—Praise my parents for a job well done. Respect them for who they are whether I agree with them or not. Lift them in prayer every day. Be there for them when they are in their twilight years.

And now I'm back to my first question. Who am I? I've changed through the years, matured, grown in wisdom, but I'm still me. I'm still that playful child chasing a ball. A loving daughter, mother, and wife. And I am confident I'm a child of God.

Dear Heavenly Father, thank you for letting me be your daughter. I am a sinner not worthy, but by grace I know I will live with You and Your Son Jesus Christ throughout eternity. Praise God. Amen.

My Talks with God

REJOICE

Beloved, do not be surprised at the fiery ordeal among you, which comes upon you for your testing, as though some strange thing were happening to you. 1 Peter 4:12 (NAS)

While dusting the top of my bookcase I ran across the pocket Bible I carried in my purse for years. It was just like the one my aunt carried in her purse. I fervently sought refuge in God's word.

After filing for divorce, the abuse became worse. I struggled knowing my Lord was not happy with divorce, and I didn't want to go against Him. In my heart I knew it was what I had to do for our safety. I felt at peace. I kept asking myself why all of this was happening. I didn't understand. In my darkest moment I opened the little black Bible and began reading. His strength and love filled my soul. Like the fishermen in open sea, I knew it was better to be in the storm with Christ than in calm water without Him.

My little Bible is so dog-eared and highlighted: but when I turn the pages, it takes me back to that lowest time in my life. I still feel His arms around me. I will always need His Word to guide me throughout my days. I hunger for His arms to hold and comfort me. I long to hear Him whisper His words of affection. Through my trials I am strengthened with God's never-ending love.

Gracious Father, thank you for Your words and Your love. Amen.

My Talks with God

UPON HIS ROCK

You also, as living stones, are being built up as a spiritual house for a holy priesthood, to offer up spiritual sacrifices acceptable to God through Jesus Christ. 1 Peter 2:5 (NAS)

I attended a Gideon meeting with my husband a few months ago, and they were talking about God, our Rock. As I listened to the verses they quoted, it made me stop and think about my life. The times I've thought about doing things on my own, I really needed to lean on God to help me through it.

Our children sing songs about building your house upon the rock. It will always stand firm. God is that Rock. He is always there to listen to your needs, wants, and most of all, your praise. He is my Rock and my Fortress, my Deliverer. I've thought about the times I got up, went about my daily grind, and didn't take time to talk to God first. Oh, things went alright, but I could feel something was amiss. Like there was a burden lying on my shoulders. A voice tugging at my side saying, "Come to me. Talk with me, walk with me, and I will give you peace through the day."

As soon as I stop, sit down, and open my Bible the feeling of elation fills my soul. I am at peace.

Gracious Heavenly Father, you are my Rock and my Redeemer. Forgive me when I start the day without you.

My Talks with God

JUDGE

God will judge both the righteous man and the wicked man for a time for every manner and for every deed is there.
Ecclesiastes 3:17 (NAS)

The other day as I sat in the car waiting for my grandson's gymnastics class to finish, I watched as a woman walked past me. Her hair was pinned on top of her head with stringy wisps blowing about her face. A dirty dress with a torn thin sweater covered her body, and a large shopping bag hung off her shoulder.

I watched as she went to the end of the building and disappeared around the corner. In the back of my mind, I thought, *What is that kind of woman doing in this neighborhood?* I froze. I just judged that woman. *What do I really know about her?*

How many times have we done the same thing without realizing we were judge and jury of someone? We do not know what is going on in another person's life. We tend to keep to ourselves not wanting to burden others with our problems so, consequently, we let our worries grow and grow until they are out of control.

A kind word, a prayer, or even a simple phrase in passing such as "How are you today?" might mean everything to them. To them it may mean someone cares. There are a lot of people who don't have a church home, a friend, or even a co-worker they can talk to. They are the ones wandering, looking, and missing the love of Jesus. We, as Christians are to share His love by that simple kind word.

Dear Father, guide me each day to utter a kind word or do something for a stranger that would make a difference in their life, to show Your love through me. Amen.

My Talks with God

PEARL OF GREAT VALUE

The kingdom of heaven is like a merchant seeking fine peals, and upon finding one pearl of great value, He went and sold all that He had and bought it. Matthew 13:45-46 (NAS)

Years ago, one of my sisters bought our mother a necklace of fine pearls. My sister told me that Mom often said she would like to have a set of pearls, so my sister saved her money for quite some time in order to buy them. When Mom showed me the pearls, her eyes lit up as she ran her fingers across each pearl. Mom never had a finer piece of jewelry.

Recently, I watched a program where they showed people diving for pearls, surfacing and diving once more to bring even more oysters to place in their buckets. The divers then searched them. More than a ton were examined to find a few quality pearls.

To our heavenly Father, each one of us is a pearl of great value. Like the pearl, He shapes and molds us every time we are in His Word. In God's eyes we are not only beautiful on the outside, but just as beautiful on the inside. 1 Peter 3:4 (NAS) says *let it be the hidden person of the heart, with the imperishable quality of a gentle and quiet spirit, which is precious in the sight of God.*

Remember each morning when you rise and each evening when you retire. You are a rare pearl.

Dear Father, thank you for making me Your pearl. Amen.

My Talks with God

WARRIOR

The Lord will go forth like a warrior. He will arouse His zeal like a man of war. He will utter a shout, yes, He will raise a war cry. He will prevail against His enemies. Isaiah 42:13 (NAS)

I've been working on a book about the Black Hawk War and found information on the ship that carried the Sauk Fax Indians from Bad Axe, Wisconsin to Jefferson Barracks, Missouri. The ship's name was *Warrior.*

Warrior was fighting for a cause. Fighting to prove a point. David, Samson, Saul, Joshua, Ahab, and Gideon were great warriors. David was a boy warrior who defeated the enemy. Gideon developed the guerilla warfare. Ahab was a warrior as well as a diplomat. Samson may have caused bedlam, but He slew many Philistines.

As children of God, we are to have a heart of a warrior. Fight the battle, spread His Word. Marilyn McCoo has a song "Warrior for the Lord." March forward, fight the injustices in the world.

Being a prayer warrior, means praying without ceasing. Pray for the homeless, famines, pray for your neighbor, and the many disasters all over the world. Pray and keep praying.

Dear Heavenly Father, comfort those who have lost their homes, their jobs, everything from the floods, tornados and wars. Give them strength help them to look skyward to You for guidance. Amen.

My Talks with God

BIBLE SCHOOL

Assemble the people, men, women and children, and the aliens living in your towns, so they can listen and learn to fear the Lord your God, and carefully follow all the words of this law.
Deuteronomy 31:12 (NIV)

I recently spotted a church sign that said we are never through with Bible school. I thought about that for only a moment and had to agree. We are never through with Bible school, Sunday School, or discipleship training. We never stop learning.

When I was young, I went to Sunday School and learned about Jonah and the whale, how Jesus fed many people, Jesus healed the sick, and the story of Noah and the big flood. The older I got, the more in depth the stories were. Now that I'm an adult, I've learned there is more to the stories. Not only did Noah and His family survive the flood, but He did so because He loved God and obeyed Him. God showed Noah His love for being righteous. Jonah tried to run from God. After being thrown into the sea, swallowed by a great fish, and finally praying to God to save him, He experienced God's love and saving grace. Jesus fed five thousand by a young boy willingly giving him his lunch of five loaves of bread and two fish. A miracle was performed that day by feeding everyone until they were full, and the left-over food filled twelve baskets. God still performs miracles today. All one needs is faith and prayer. Pray believing that your prayers will be answered. My God is a loving God who wants what is best for His children. We, you and I, are God's children. How blessed we are.

Dear Father in Heaven, thank you for calling me Your child. Amen.

My Talks with God

GREAT LIFE

When Christ, who is your life, appears then you also will appear with Him in glory. Colossians 3:4 (NIV)

While talking to my eight-year-old grandson, he told me they were going to have a play day at school. "We're having a water splash, eat pizza, have a roller coaster, just everything, Grandma."

I said, "You're going to be out of school pretty soon. I guess this is the end-of-year party?"

His reply was, "Oh, yes, Grandma, then I'm going to the pool, Sea World, Six Flags, Schlitterbahn, and then I'm going to Disney World at Christmas."

I couldn't help but chuckle. "You're going to have a busy summer."

"Yes, Grandma. I have a great life."

How many times have we told ourselves we have a great life? We think about our possessions, how much money is in our bank account, and the vacations we take. We are the spoiled children of God. We have a good life. Most of us have good health, loving spouses, a roof over our heads, money to pay our bills, and we have friends who are there to lift us up in prayer when we are down?

But how many think about our lives, really think about the life God gave us? He gave us life to follow Him, to share His Word and stand in glory with Him. Lead others to His wonderous love, everlasting life, mercy and grace. God's grace. He loved us so much that He gave His only son to die for our sins. How much can we do for Him?

Dear Father in Heaven, thank you for giving Your Son for my sins and my life. I will forever be in Your debt. I will never be able to do enough for You. Thank you. Amen.

My Talks with God

MY NAME IS "I AM"

And those who know Your name will put their trust in You; for you, Lord, have never forsaken those who seek You. Psalms 9:10 (NIV)

On Easter Sunday our two daughters came to church with their families. They don't do this often enough. My eight-year-old grandson sat on one side and the five-year-old grandson sat on the other. Usually the eight-year-old sits with his parents, so this was a treat for me. It was the first time for the five-year-old grandson.

During one song, my eight-year-old asked me who were they singing about. "Was it Ya-Who-Ya?" I tried not to laugh at what he thought he heard and explained it was Yahweh. Another word to describe Lord or Jesus.

Later in the service he asked another question, then another. I said a silent prayer thanking God for speaking to my grandson's heart.

Not long after, I attended a ladies' Bible study that focused on names of our Lord and what they meant. Jehoval-Nissi, the Lord My Banner. Jehovah-Jireh, the Lord will Provide. Elohim, Creator. El Elyon, the Most High God. Jehovah-Shalom, the Lord is Peace. Jehovah-Sabaoth, the Lord is Peace. Jehovah-Rapha, the Lord that healeth. El Olam, the Everlasting God.

My God is the great healer, the Lord of Lords, the great Creator, and He provides me with all I need.

Heavenly Father, thank you for being my everything. I am most blessed to have you as my all in all. Amen.

My Talks with God

STAND FAST

Not that we lord it over your faith, but we work with you for your joy, because it is by faith you stand firm. II Corinthians 1:24 (NIV)

It's so easy to get caught up in the day-to-day things that go on in our lives. We tell ourselves just this once. I've been working hard all week, I'm tired, and even the excuse of "I deserve a day for me." Before you know it, we are out at the lake on a picnic, or just sleeping in on Sunday morning.

Then one time leads to two, then three, and it gets harder to break the cycle. You wake up one day and you can't remember the last time you attended church. You've convinced yourself that God still loves you. He's not a bad God; you're not a bad person.

No, our God is not a bad God. He is a loving God full of grace and mercy. But He is also a God that asks His people to stand fast in our faith. To praise and worship Him on the Sabbath. Prayer for each other gives strength to all. Together we can remain faithful until Christ's return.

Dear Father, thank you for Your love. Forgive me when I fail You. Amen

My Talks with God

FOLLOW YOUR HEART

Ruth said, "Do not urge me to leave you or turn back from following you, for where you go, I will go, and where you lodge, I will lodge. Your people shall be my people, and your God, my God."
Ruth 1:16 (NAS)

I was with a group of writers a few weeks ago and someone told me they didn't feel comfortable changing their story to fit the audience. If they did, then it wouldn't be their story. I asked her what was her heart telling her to do. I told her I would follow my heart.

I had that same problem with one of my stories, too. My story still lays in a box, and it will stay there until I feel comfortable finishing it. When my heart tells me it is time.

Ruth followed her heart when she went with her mother-in-law. She knew this was the right choice, what God wanted her to do.

Similar struggles pull on our hearts every day whether we realize it or not. You might say it's our conscience telling us to do something. A seed is planted then our subconscious takes over. Do we do this certain thing, or do we let it go? A tug of war ensues.

A group of children are at play when one suggests they do some mischief. One child knows this isn't right but is afraid to say anything. His heart, or conscience, starts to bother him, telling him, "No you shouldn't do this." There again, another tug of war within.

The bottom line is, follow what your heart is telling you. Some still may say it's your conscience, but I'd like to think God speaks to me through my heart. I know right from wrong, when someone needs a hug, a kind word, or even when to keep my mouth shut. Through His grace and spirit, God touches me and lets me know what to do. I like to think it's through my heart.

Heavenly Father, thank you for letting me know when You are with me guiding me, through my heart. Amen.

My Talks with God

MY OLD DAYS

And as for you, you shall go to your fathers in peace; you shall be buried at a good old age. Genesis 15:15 (NAS)

Hello, Lord. Here I am again. Yes, today is one of my old days again. You know what I mean. Not that I'm feeling old, but I guess what I'm trying to say, I feel overwhelmed. I want to slow things down so I can get more things done. Give me more hours in the day maybe.

I get up early enough, make the bed, start a load of laundry, feed the dogs, and my day begins. It's one thing then another. The phone rings taking up my time, time I set aside to do what I need to get done and what I wished I could get done.

By noon I feel like I could take a nap but know I must push forward. On to still another chore and before you know it, it's time to fix dinner.

I know, Lord, I'm complaining again. I have so much to be thankful for. Why, if it weren't for my good health, I wouldn't be getting up each day to hear the birds sing or see the trees blowing in the wind. I'd miss the fragrant sweet smell of the roses at my front door, much less, be able to clean and cook for the day.

Lord, I just miss being able to do things faster. You know, like I used to be able to do when I was twenty or even thirty. You say it's my time to slow down and bask in Your Glory. Reflect on my life and let You take my hand and lead me. You know that's hard, Father. I'm still trying to stay in control. I forget you are the Master.

Thank you, Father, for reminding me that You are the One in command of my life. I surrender each morning to you when I arise and continually throughout the day. You guide me. I may not be able to take the steps two at a time, but each step I take You are with me. Amen.

My Talks with God

AM I READY?

Nation will rise against nation, and kingdom against kingdom. And there will be great earthquakes in various places, and famines and pestilences, and there will be fearful sights and great signs from heaven. Luke 21:10-11 (NAS)

I received an e-mail the other day asking if I was ready for Jesus' return. They cited the current wars, earthquakes, tsunamis, famines, terrorists, floods, tornados, hurricanes, and the list goes on.

Jesus said these things would all happen before His return. But He also said the Son of Man is coming at an hour you do not expect.

What He is saying is that we are to be faithful and have patience. We are to pursue righteousness and gentleness. As He said all along, treat your neighbors as you would treat yourself, always. Keep the Ten Commandments every day. Pray and seek God's guidance for your life. Help those who hunger, hunger for food and for God's message.

Yes, there have been more frequent earthquakes, more floods and hurricanes than in the past. There will always be wars and rumors of wars. It will continue until man can learn to live together and love each other. And that will be when Christ returns.

So, the question remains. Am I ready? Do I keep God's Commandments? Do I seek His guidance and keep Him first and foremost in my daily life? Am I in His Word daily? Are you?

Dear Heavenly Father, thank you for Your promise to return and take Your children home to live with You forever. Amen.

My Talks with God

SHOW DON'T TELL

May those who wait for Thee not be ashamed through me, O Lord God of hosts: May those who seek Thee not be dishonored through me, O God of Israel. Psalm 69:6 (NAS)

As a writer I tell other writers to show me what they are wanting to say, not tell me. It makes a better story to show someone, draw a picture, scene, etc., rather than tell them what is going on. Sometimes I need to be reminded of that, too.

As a Christian, I also need to be aware there are others watching how I live my life. God expects me to live as Christ lived His.

I must guard my tongue against petty gossip and running down another person to make myself look better. As Jesus said, "I will come into temptation, the spirit is willing, but the flesh is weak." I can only be an example by reading God's Word every day and asking for His help.

I must guard my eyes against all idols and anything that is detestable in God's sight. I must restrain my feet from every evil way so that I may keep God's Word.

I must use my hands to help others whether in crisis or not. To give a hug when needed or a pat on the back for a job well done. I must use my ears to listen to the pain and hurt of others.

And last, but not least, my heart needs to be like the heart of Jesus Christ. Love like He loves. Forgive like He forgives. Through Him all things are possible. You may not feel like you can do these things but when you ask Him for help, He is there. You can do all things through Jesus Christ our Lord and Savior.

Dear Father, please hear my prayer and give me a heart for others so I may love like You. Amen.

My Talks with God

Pathway to God's Plan of Salvation

1. Romans 5:8 God loves you

[8] But God demonstrates his own love for us in this: While we were still sinners, Christ died for us.

2. Romans 3:10-12 All have sinned—He still loves you

[10] As it is written: "There is no one righteous, not even one;
[11] there is no one who understands; there is no one who seeks God.
[12] All have turned away, they have together become worthless; there is no one who does good, not even one.

3. John 3:16 God's love sent His Son into the world

[16] For God so loved the world that he gave his one and only Son, that whoever believes in him shall not perish but have eternal life.

4. John 15:13-14 His love is seen in Jesus

[13] Greater love has no one than this: to lay down one's life for one's friends. [14] You are my friends if you do what I command.

5. Romans 6:23 His love paid the wages of your sin

[23] For the wages of sin is death, but the gift of God is eternal life in Christ Jesus our Lord.

6. Revelation 3:20 His love is knocking at your heart through Jesus

[20] Here I am! I stand at the door and knock. If anyone hears my voice and opens the door, I will come in and eat with that person, and they with me.

7. Romans 15:13 His love will flood your life when you accept Jesus as your Savior

[13] May the God of hope fill you with all joy and peace as you trust in him, so that you may overflow with hope by the power of the Holy Spirit.

Remember

Everyone who calls on the name of the Lord will be saved.
Romans 10:13

PRAY THIS PRAYER

"Lord Jesus, I am a sinner. Lord, forgive me. I know you died for me and that you rose again. I want you to come into my life and fill it with your Spirit. Thank you, Lord Jesus, for eternal life."

All verses for Plan of Salvation taken from the NIV.

Made in the USA
Monee, IL
18 September 2023

42929719R00063